BEHIND CLOSED DOORS

MARRIED

TO THE

Church

MY WIFE IS MY MISTRESS

DR RICHELLE RESTO

Behind Closed Door's visual image is a quick concise introduction to all of the private things that pastors and their wives encounter outside the doors of the church. These images will give meaning to what's done in the dark that will be made manifest by the light.

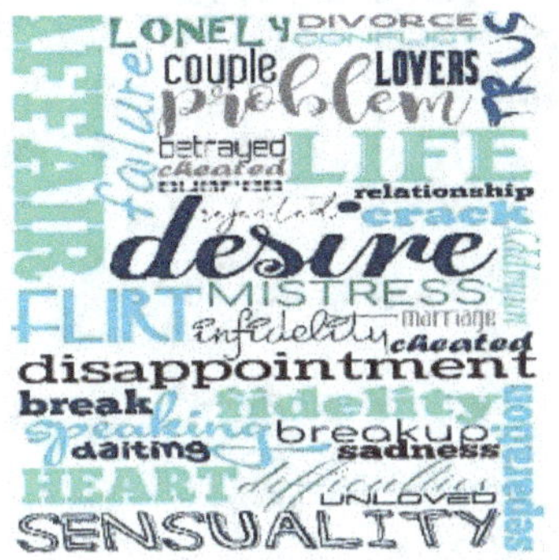

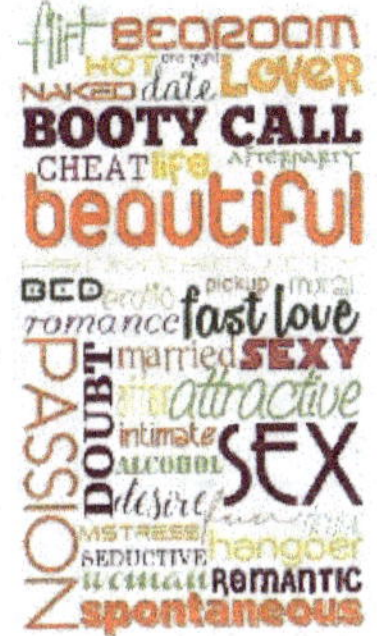

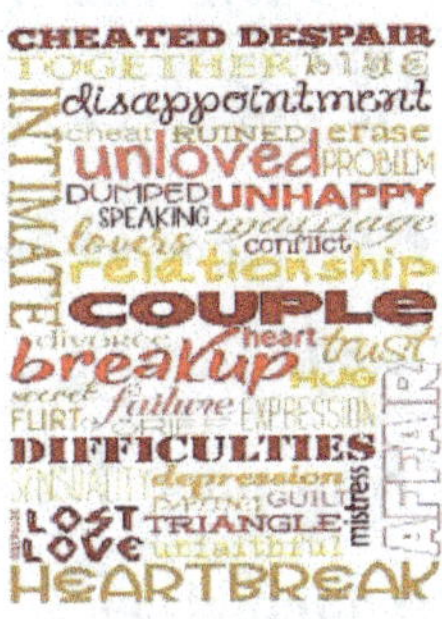

Behind closed doors

Table of Contents

Dedication 6

Acknowledgment......7

Introduction 9

Every open door must be closed......10

Infidelity......15

The vow......22

Denial 25

People pleasing......30

Frustration......34

Emotionalism......36

Restoration......39

Revenge......42

Intimacy......46

Guilt......48

Misery 50

Transparency 53

Practice what you preach! 58

Ultimatums 61

Reflections 64

Private Collection of Poetry...... 65

There is a Sequel Coming 66

About the Author 67

Dedication

To all of the leaders, pastors, leading ladies, and elect ladies that I've encountered over the years, who have suffered in silence and didn't have a platform: This book is written for you.

Acknowledgment

Throughout the rigorous period of completing this project, many individuals assisted me behind closed doors. My candid appreciation goes to Joy and Jachelle for the endless support, and above all, their patience with me when I teetered along the path of uncertainty and insurmountable challenges. Finally, a special thanks goes to April McMillan, Lila Adams, Marcia Chiles, and Karen Durant. Y'all have been my friends, colleagues, shoulder to cry on, and confidants in this ordeal. Thank you all for paving the way for me to follow.

My sincere gratitude goes to my family and friends for reminding me about the most important things in life. Your unconditional love and support meant the world to me.

Thank YOU

Many times, pastors in leadership positions have many roles inside and outside the church. They tend to enjoy having the admiration they receive in the church and ignore the people that love them behind closed doors. This book provides personal insights into the lives of some pastors, and how they treat their wives behind closed doors. Many wives have had to learn how to triumph over years of pain, fight through the tears and overcome their reality as they live with men who are married to the church.

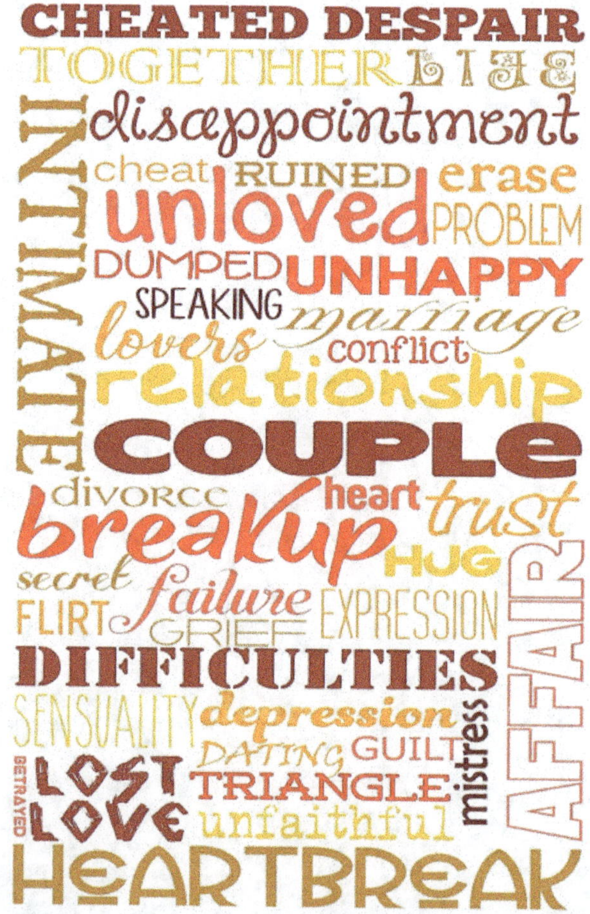

Chapter 1

Every open door must be closed

As I sat in my Jeep in front of the Lifetime gym parking lot and reminiscing about how I met my husband fifteen years ago and waiting to confront him about all of the matters at hand. After all, he was the one who broke my heart, and then selfishly left me to go to the church. It was obvious that he had abandoned our dreams. He was supposed to love me unconditionally. He was supposed to be my everything.

My mind always reflects where it all began. The signs that he was cheating on me became obvious early after we began our relationship in 1993. I received a phone call from April, my sister, telling me about the high school football game she had attended. "Destiny, *the score was 0 to 38, the other team got destroyed and I loved it!" April told me joyfully. However, it was her next words that almost stopped my heart. "You'll never guess who I saw at the game though, I'm sorry to be the one telling you about this, however, I saw Roger with another woman, and they did not look like they were just friends!"*

As my sister described everything she observed between Mark and this woman, my heart began to beat in a frantic rhythm. Myriads of thoughts spun in my mind and I felt like I was having an out-of-body experience. My phone hit the floor, as tears ran down my face. Before I knew it, I had flung the college dorm's door and was racing down five flights of stairs. I was living the worst nightmare of my life.

I paused when I started throwing up on my black striped bodycon skinny playsuit jumper and red stilettos, but it wasn't for long. "Why is this happening to me?" were the words I shouted at God. "Why is this happening to me?" I shouted at Marcia, the residential counselor who seemingly came out of nowhere after hearing all the commotion in the hallway. Everything inside me was screaming and I had no choice but to voice my thoughts. I looked into the heavens above and yelled, "I

9

can't do this anymore!"

Fifteen years later, I was still dealing with what I said I couldn't handle. Usually, I would have parked my baby; a metallic black-on-black 2007 Jeep, Chrysler 300C with twenty-two-inch rims and limo type tinted windows on the driveway, but instead, I parked in a secluded spot in the back of Panera bread to shroud myself in complete darkness. I allowed my mind to wander a bit, totally oblivious of the outside world and its problems. My life as a pastor's wife should be simple and plain but it wasn't; I had problems like everyone else. No amount of money spent on toys, no amount of time or sweat wasted away in the gym, and no matter how far I ran, drove, or flew, my problems were not going away.

The churning and tugging in my stomach were enough to make me want to open the car and surrender the half-eaten plate of salad I gulped down during lunch. After a couple of slow agonizing minutes, accompanied by a few steady deep breaths, the sickening feeling reluctantly passed. I was too tired to give it a second thought and at that point, I was concerned about getting home. My husband kept dialing my phone and I just let it go to voicemail. I had a meeting with another of my husband's mistresses for dinner at Red Lobsters, so I ignored it! My stomach lurched as I stepped out of my car and simply refused to let go. For that brief moment, the words I had said fifteen years ago echoed through my mind, *God, I can't do this anymore, I cried immensely. Please, help me close this door of misery.* I got back in the car and sat there behind the wheel shroud in complete darkness due to the blacked-out windows and allowed my mind to wander a bit, totally oblivious to the outer world and its problems. That night, I stayed at the Renaissance hotel, for fear of facing the truth, that my husband was married to God and his mistresses too. After getting off the elevator, I was looking for Room 888 which was symbolic of a new beginning. I ignored it and just opened the door and began to cry, scream out words of anger, hurt, and pains, it so much that I was unable to discern my thoughts. It was dark and I was in the valley of misery and lacked self-awareness. All of these negative thoughts ran through my mind. For hours, I just sat on the floor trying to get some self-control, understanding and organizing my thoughts. I was trying to get in touch with my feelings but deep down, I was mad as Hell. See, Behind this Door is the real me and my worst enemy. For me to deal with everyone on the outside, I had to be in touch with my feelings, and this relationship was affecting me emotionally. Behind Closed

Doors, I was making judgments about myself, my husband, and all of his mistresses; Tanya, Camilla, Aerin, Latoya, and this last one penned down in history, the Church and then there was Me.

I lacked self-control and any degree of self-awareness

I was unconscious of my behavior, actions or attitudes

I lacked sensitivity and alienated myself from them ever hurting me again

I placed unnecessary barriers that impacted my mannerisms towards clichés, people and even the church.

Moments before I drifted off to sleep on the hotel floor, these simple words came whispering inside of me, *This VALLEY will never be your final Destination. You may wallow in a puddle of tears, but God will close this door and give you New Beginnings and total Victory! God is watching you and allowing you to sleep in the bosom of his arms tonight! This is Your Exodus, Now Allow GOD to close the Door! Rest my child, rest. Behind the Closed Door of Desperation.*

A couple of months later, dressed in my gym attire, I hit the trunk release button as I exited my car to retrieve my duffle bag and go for a 30-minute workout at the Lifetime gym. I was feeling good these days because after confronting my husband and slapping the taste out of his mouth, he was back to his loving self and preaching like a storm. On September 23, 2004, things began to fall apart after the Wednesday night Executive Board meeting. My husband told me, "stay at home and get some rest" but something told me I needed to be at this particular meeting. Being the submissive and doting wife, I stayed at home and prayed... *"Lord, I don't know what this nausea feeling is, but please cover my family and don't allow us to suffer because of his past mistakes and secret sins."* Then the kitchen house phone rang, and I thought it was my husband calling to tell me about the meeting. But, it was the church secretary crying uncontrollably. I told her to calm down and tell me what happened.

First Lady, it was the most uncomfortable meeting that I had to record. At the meeting, they told Pastor to sit down and Chairmen Ramon will be leading the meeting. Chairmen Ramon began to tell the board that a strange woman called the church asking for a return call about Pastor. Deacon Ted shared that they found out about the mistress because she left a voicemail message on the church phone. Deacon Ted played the detailed recording, showed pictures and shared the information with the entire board. My mind drifted and I was thinking that this has been resolved, how will that heifer dare do that after I paid her five hundred dollars to get rid of the baby. *First Lady, Secretary La'Chonne shouted, Are you still there? Did you hear anything that I just said to you?* Sorry, La'Chonne I stated, I blanked out for a moment and kneeled on the kitchen floor. *What else happened at the meeting?* I replied. *Secretary La'chonne said, they voted to suspend Pastor for a couple of Sundays without pay and he stormed out of the meeting. I'm sorry to tell you this, but I felt that you needed to know.* I replied, thank you Sister La'chonne and have a great night. On the kitchen floor, I said *Lord, not our will, but may your will be done! Grant me the serenity to deal with this man and the pain that you gave to me!*

When my husband came home at 9:00 pm, I could tell that something was wrong from the look in his eyes and his black suit looked messed up. I asked him *"how did things go at the meeting?"* There was anger in his voice, he was shouting words of hatred, dismay, discontent, blaming me for not handling his mistress or taking better care of him at home; It was all my fault. His passive-aggressive behaviors were beginning to get on my nerves and I just let the words roll off my back and sat in silence for the next two hours.

After a month of sleepless nights, my husband was back to preaching at the church and we were back on schedule. I walked towards the trunk, the feelings of nausea resurfaced. Bright flashes of immense light exploded before my eyes, leaving blinking red spots in their wake. I stumbled as the lightheadedness and double vision that preceded the blinding lights sent my two hundred and thirty-pound frame to one knee. I braced myself with one hand on the wet, sticky pavement and waited for the wave of sickness to run its course. After what seemed like an eternity, my world righted itself and normal vision reluctantly returned. I regained my composure after a few deep breaths and reclaimed my weary body.

From a humbled warrior's position, I stood and whispered encouraging words to myself to go on. I was having a meeting with another of my husband's mistresses at the Lifetime gym for several hours to avoid running into anyone that would know me or my business. Fifteen years of marriage and I still had to clean up after my husband, the honorable man of God that was providing more than spiritual leadership to several female members of the church. His duties involved laying on of hands, preparing weekly sermons, preaching and conducting worship services, but he also assisted with the management of all women's ministries.

My husband's adulterous behavior was the basis of my meeting with his latest mistress who called herself Destiny. You see, when my husband is 'done' with a mistress, he sends me in to quietly get rid of her by any means necessary. As his first lady, I have no choice but to follow his orders. Anytime I'm forced to have these meetings, I make it a point to learn all of the intimate details that led to their relationship so that I can report back to the leading ladies of the church. That way, they have all the tools they need to correctly manage their husbands with wandering eyes. In a perfect world, these men would not stray from their marriages and as women, we shouldn't tolerate that type of disrespect but sadly, we chose to stay and deal with it.

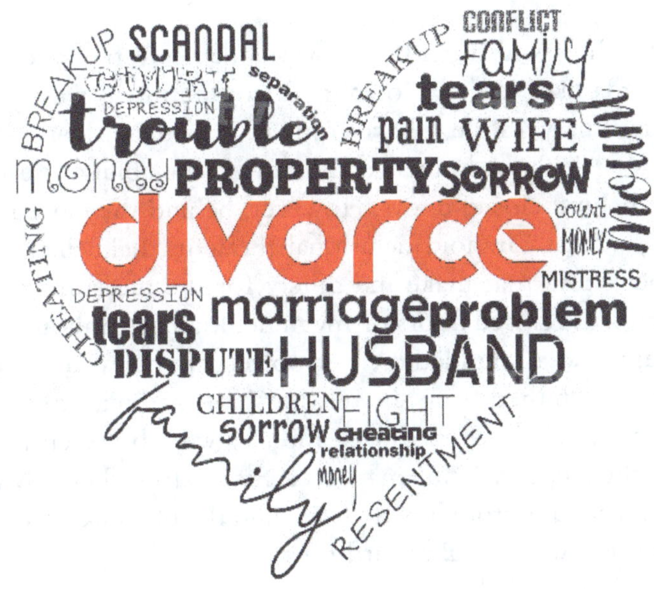

Chapter 2
Infidelity

My name is Destiny, AKA Diamond, and I was born with a desire not to be restricted to one person and I love men of power. I am a talented young woman that has a narcissistic core that dictates gratification and attention to my needs. I have been under the care of different psychiatrists, practically, all of my life. I was diagnosed with having a Schizophreniform disorder and I've been hospitalized several times over the years.

My relationships with men have always been care-free and at the age of 33, words like 'settling down' and 'commitment' were not a part of my vocabulary. In life, I have come to realize that being someone's mistress was all about influence and having the ability to exercise my influence behind closed doors. However, behind the closed doors of my mind, I have paranoid delusional thoughts, hallucinations, and I display behaviors that make me thirsty for the pleasures of married men. Behind the closed doors of my mind, I fantasize about how to get strong but yet weak-minded men of power into my web of deception. All of these stemmed from the relationship I had with my stepfather; that particular relationship caused me to always be resentful towards men and their needs. I put my needs first before theirs. My current lover is a married pastor named Roger, and the pleasure of hooking up with him was a wonderful reward for me.

When I first met the odious Pastor Roger Frederick in 2009 at the Lifetime Gym, it didn't take much time for me to see that he was my type; weak-minded and he needed a fun-loving, bossy, adventurous, daring and classy side chick in his life. When I first saw him, it was easy to spot his fake bravado as he walked into the gym. I knew he was going to be my next victim. I could tell by his demeanor that he was a wanderer but had not lived on the edge. He was a smooth talker, tough, handsome, smooth-talking, clean cut. But, I noticed an air of indecisiveness and he had no capacity for danger. All the perfect signs to be my prey.

Roger caught the attention of almost all the ladies at the gym. As I observed him engaging in a conversation with the gym instructor, I began to fantasize about where our first meeting would be; should we do dinner at a popular restaurant or should I invite him over? I was working the details out in my mind as I slowly walked on the treadmill. I felt a sense of confidence as he took a spot right across from me, putting himself in my area of focus. I wasted no time; I made eye contact and he waved in response. I winked and smiled to let him know he had my attention. I adjusted my shirt slightly to reveal a bit of my cleavage, and I gave him seductive looks and continued to smile so that he knew I was into him. Once the class was over, I made my way over to him to introduce myself.

"Hi, I'm Destiny," I said.

"I'm Roger," he replied. "It's very nice to meet you."

We walked out of the gym together in full conversation and by the time we got to his car, he offered me a ride home and I happily accepted. The ride was pleasant and once he got me home, I gave him a seductive smile as I said, "thank you," and went into the house. About an hour later, he called me because I intentionally left my wallet behind in his car, therefore, he had no choice but to reach out to me. By the time he arrived, I had changed into the sexiest lingerie gown I had. It was red, showed a lot of cleavages and it was tight in all the right places, showing off all of my curves and skin. I let my hair flow down my back and kept my makeup on neutral so the only thing left to do was to turn him on and out. That was the plan as I patiently awaited his arrival.

An hour later, he was ringing my doorbell and I was set to surprise him at the door too, I watched his expression turned from surprise to lust within seconds of opening the door and I was elated. I thanked him for bringing back my wallet and offered him a cup of coffee. He accepted. We sat in my living room and had a light conversation while he wantonly stared at my heaving cleavage. It tickled me to see that my seductive tactics were working on him. I purposely moved closer so that he could get a better look and almost leaned in close enough to get a kiss. We were interrupted by his cell phone ringing. As he looked to see who was calling, he glanced at me and said that he had somewhere to be. I walked him to his car, hugged him and let him go. Not long after, Roger texted me not only to let me know he got home safely but that he also wanted to see me the next day. I accepted and sent him a smiley face text message.

From that moment on, the possibility of being with him dominated my thoughts. I wanted him desperately. I fantasized about his body on mine, his skin close to mine, our sweat beads and body fluids combining, became my beautiful dream. I couldn't wait to have him, my next conquest. The next day finally came and I started my day off by going to the gym. I decided to keep my activities light as I was looking forward to seeing Roger later that day. As I walked on the treadmill, I fantasized about Roger and all that I had planned for him. I was so deep into my daydream that I almost didn't hear my phone ringing. Roger's call brought me back to reality.

"Hi, Angel," he whispered on the phone. "I trust you had a good night's rest. Hope to see you at 1 pm."

"I can't wait! See you then," I replied.

I dashed into the bathroom to take a cold shower and then get dressed for my date. A tight Red fitted dress, a little bit of Mac flawless shade 44 foundation with a pop of ruby red lipstick and black stilettos heel was all that I needed to seduce Pastor Roger.

An hour later, Roger pulled his 2009 black tinted Mercedes Benz near my front steps and called to let me know he was outside. I took one last look in the dresser mirror then exited my front door in a slow, sexy walk toward his car. He stepped out to open the door for me, all the while taking in everything I was serving.

"You look stunning," he said as I got in the car.

I smiled wickedly and said, "I'm exactly what you ordered."

He took me to the fanciest soul food restaurant in town called Sylvia's and we had the best time; eating, drinking and discussing many topics including the fact that he was married and a pastor. Immediately, I wondered about his wife. *Did she know what he was doing and who he was doing it with?* Not that I cared because I planned to seduce him but still, it made me wonder if she was the type of woman who tolerated her man sleeping around. It didn't matter to me, I planned to rock Roger's world. After dinner, Roger suggested we see a movie and I agreed. We chose a romantic comedy and once we were in the theatre, we picked a secluded area. Every chance we got, we flirted with each other and kisses were exchanged. I was completely confident that I had Roger exactly where I wanted him.

After the movie, he drove me home and of course, I asked him to come in and have a cup of coffee with me. He happily accepted. While the coffee was brewing, I changed into a sexy nightgown. My bosom bounced as I brought him the coffee and he couldn't take his eyes off me. *Oh yes, I got you now!* I mused as I handed him the coffee and sat next to him. As he took the cup out of my hand, I started to loosen his tie.

"Let me help you get comfortable," I told him, smiling.

This move allowed me to go closer and plant a kiss on his succulent lips. He hungrily returned my kiss and before I knew it, his hands were all over me, pulling up my pink satin nightgown, kissing my neck and going downtown. Letting me know exactly what he wanted to do to me next. I almost lost concentration when he grabs my hands but I just continued to avoid looking into his eyes. For a brief moment, my thoughts became cloudy and I was inflamed with guilt but driven by lust, power, control, and vulnerability. I needed this man inside and on top of me to erase all of the fear, doubt, and unbelief. I knew it was a lie, but tonight he will fulfill my sexual reality. Tonight, this was "all about me."

"Let's take this to my bedroom," I said and Roger was more to comply with my request. I smiled wickedly as I congratulated myself for yet another successful conquest.

Pastor Roger didn't leave my house until the next day and even though I told him I would see him again, I didn't intend to. I only wanted one night with him because that's all I needed and, to be honest, that's all a married man can give me. Next, I was my only thought. I never looked back at used goods. Some call me Jezebel, but I call myself a Conqueror!

Sunday morning rolled back around quickly, and I had a new man in sight. As I got dressed for church, I thought about who I would meet because I was going to a church that a friend recommended. Apparently, her church was having a 5th-anniversary celebration and I knew there would be a new conquest among the parishioners. Of course, Pastor Roger kept calling me, but his calls went straight to voicemail. He was now in my past, therefore I was done with him. Once I was satisfied with my look, I got into my car and headed to my friend's church. It didn't take long to spot the pastor of her church as he was standing in front of the church when I got there. He was very handsome but also had a serious look which made me think I might have to work harder to get him. Sitting in church next to my friend, my focus was on the pastor as he preached but his captivating sermon had me thinking that he might not be easy to conquer. I had no plans on giving up though. The service was uplifting to the end and I truly enjoyed it but at the same time, I had a goal to accomplish so my focus never changed.

"Did you enjoy the service?" my friend Mary asked me.

"Yes, I did. I would love to worship here."

After I responded, I realized how I sounded and pulled back a bit as I didn't want to give Mary any hints of my true intentions.

"That's great! Let me introduce you to the pastor," Mary said as she walked towards the pastor. Excitedly, I followed her lead.

By the time we arrived at Pastor Mark's side, he was still saying his goodbyes to everyone but still took a minute to talk to us.

"Hello, Pastor Mark. As always, I felt that anointing and I pray it never runs dry," Mary said.

"Hello Mary, it's always good to see you and I see you've brought a new parishioner with you. I do hope you enjoyed this morning's sermon as well," Pastor Mark said and I took it as my cue to introduce myself.

"Yes, I did enjoy it very much. My name is Destiny and it's a pleasure to meet you." I extended my hand and he did the same. I held his hand a bit longer as a way to flirt with him a bit.

"Nice to meet you Destiny. You are welcome to our sanctuary and if you ever need someone to talk with, I'm available. Here's my card. My office is always open."

As he handed me his card, I smiled, knowing that was the first step to getting exactly what I wanted. "Thank you, Pastor Mark, you will be hearing from me," I said with a hint of deception, hoping he would catch my drift.

"You're welcome Destiny and I will see you soon. Mary, I look forward to seeing you for the weekly services as well," Pastor Mark said as he walked off to talk with other parishioners.

"Thank you, Pastor Mark!" Mary and I said in unison.

I said goodbye to my friend and headed home with thoughts of conquering Pastor Mark.

Once I was home, I looked at the card Mark gave me and saw that along with an office number, there was also a cell phone number, so I decided to send him a text. He responded very religiously which totally threw me off, but I had no intention of giving up on him. I went about the rest of my day as though nothing happened.

The next day, which was Monday morning, I called Mary to see about us going to bible study; I need more time to figure Mark out. She agreed for us to meet at a restaurant for lunch before bible study and I had no problem with that. I arrived at our favorite lunch spot first and as I placed my order, I spotted a well-dressed man staring at me while quietly sitting at a table by himself. He was wearing a clergy collar and a wedding band. *My kind of man* I thought as I walked towards him. I introduced myself and asked him if I could sit with him. He responded in the affirmative and I sat down with a smile.

"My name is Destiny. Thank you for allowing me to sit with you." I said to him.

"I'm Pastor Steven, so nice to meet you," he said with a welcoming smile.

Within five minutes, I found out that he was new in town. He had arrived alone, but his family would be arriving soon. Naturally, I offered to show him around town and be available for any of his *needs*. My offer made him smile and we immediately exchanged phone numbers. Time flew so quickly that I didn't realize that Mary never showed up for our lunch date and just when I was about to call her, Steven surprised me by asking me out to dinner later that night.

"I tell you what, why don't we have dinner at my house?" I asked. "I'll cook you a delicious home-cooked meal. I'm sure it's been a while since you've had one." I quietly congratulated myself for thinking so quickly.

"I accept. Write down your address for me," Steven said.

I quickly jotted down my address.

Later that night, I made baked chicken, steamed rice, and mashed potatoes. While dinner was cooking, I took a long bath, got dressed. Pastor Steven arrived on time and I directed him to the living room area while I served dinner. In the living room, he was quietly reading his sermons and I came out of the kitchen with two hot plates of food while wearing my skin-tight red nightgown. His eyes bulged out of the sockets as he watched me walk toward him which was a clear indication that I had him where I wanted him. Steven, Mark, Roger, and many more like them will fall for my plot, eat what I serve and drink whatever I have them swallow. That was my claim to fame, Behind the Doors of the Mistress.

Chapter 3
The vow

I smiled widely as I glanced at my backyard from my seat on the patio. You've got it made, Destiny, I told myself proudly and was living my best life for a long time. Dating different men, getting gifts, going on trips, and endless sex, that was my whole life and I enjoyed every minute of it. Girlfriends or wives never meant anything to me and why should they? I did not commit these men, I had no reason to be honest or loyal; I was doing me and that's all I cared about until the day I met the man who is now my husband, Mark.

Mark was a devoted Christian and even though I've met and slept with many men who called themselves devoted Christians, I felt Mark was different from the rest, and he wanted to save the best for last. Although I tried to check out the package underneath his tight clothes, he maintained his commitment and vow to the Lord. He was a true man of God that could do no wrong. He was educated with a degree in Pastoral ministry, anointed, hilarious and incredibly sexy, smart and he has a bronze six-feet-two-inch athletic body. His charismatic attitude, scripture reading baritone voice and sense of security had me trapped and before I knew it, I was not only in love, but I also wanted to leave my inappropriate behavior in the distance. I turned over a new leaf and ready to change my player name from Destiny to First Lady N'dia.

After my former lifestyle, I became the kind of woman that I knew Mark had to marry. I knew it wouldn't be easy but based on the kind of man of God Mark was and the healthy conversations I had with my friend, Lora, who was a marriage counselor, I was able to develop and grow into the woman I am today.

Lora and I met at a professional leadership conference. I was having a hard time finding a session to attend and sat in the lobby area beside Lora. Lora had such a kind demeanor and sweet spirit. I guess she could tell by the look on my face that I was struggling emotionally, adjusting to not only this conference but in my personal life too;

dating an anointed man of God while I was still struggling with a sinful lifestyle. Well, transitioning from being a sinner to a saint. Lora reminded me of my grandmother but she had dark features like Cecily Tyson and a terrible wig that needed some glue on both sides. But, her voice sounded like Maya Angelo when she leaned over and said, Sugar, *God said, everything is going to be alright.* I burst out in tears and this lady held me and prayed for two hours in a public lobby area. The more she prayed I tried to get away, but she held me tighter until I felt God washing my sins away. Right there in that lobby area, God delivered me from my hellish ways. From that day, Lora took me under her wings and empowered me to be the best woman that I could be. Lora was my angel and she opened my eyes to become self-conscious about my decisions, and she was the only confidant that could build my self-esteem and never allowed fear to paralyze my next destination. After many sessions, she learned about Destiny, Diamond, and now First Lady N'dia but never judged me based on my past.

Mark and I had a wonderful 10 months courtship and we never discussed my past and just focused on our future. In my mind, that is why I had Lora to share my past secrets with and he didn't need to know about Diamond or Destiny. My life motto was *"You can't let the left hand know what the right hand has done."* Although Lora suggested that I never go into a marriage with secrets, especially, after finding multiple hotel receipts in his car glove compartment, condoms in his side drawer under the bible, and a locked box in his closet with no key in sight. So, I concluded that it was best to leave the past in the past and Mark would share his secrets when he was ready.

In October 2015, Mark would begin his journey as a Pastor of Markham Chapel Baptist Church and I knew that things were getting pretty serious between us. After 10 months of dating, on an impromptu day trip to Virginia Beach, he gave me a map and told me that he is going to give me the world and that I must promise to never leave him despite all of his weaknesses, flaws, and shortcomings. I knew Mark had skeletons in his closet that I wasn't ready to address, but I was blinded by love and attracted to the power of his anointing. You know what they say, the *"Anointing destroys yokes."* That I ignored all of the red flags and was so excited to spend the rest of my life with a man that never entered into my promise land or tasted the forbidden fruit. So, I said *Yes, Mark, I will never leave you or forsake you, you are my Boo!* I was still in the moment when he kissed me passionately and pressed against my body. My God, this man set my soul on fire. If we weren't on the beach in this public area, I would have laid hands on him and the two would have become one. But, he stopped and said I can't wait until you carry my last name. My private thoughts said, *"No he didn't,"* he got me *purring like a cat, cobwebs in the promised land and he stops in the midst of me getting ready to put my Diamond moves on him."* He is such a gentleman, he grabbed my hands, held me close while we watched the waves for the rest of the day.

When Mark proposed at my favorite seafood and jazz restaurant, I was filled with joy. That night was so special because the sky was pretty blue and it seemed like the heavens opened up for me. Tears flowed down my face as I happily said yes to his proposal. As soon as Mark put the ring on my finger, I called everyone and blasted the good news on my social media accounts. During our courting time, I joined Mark's church, gave my life to Christ, joined the choir, women's axillary and became very involved in the church's activities. It seems people in the church didn't know we were engaged. But, I didn't care because I was blinded by love and I was the prize, his good thing and favor from the Lord.

Over the years, I learned about all the things I needed to know about being a pastor's wife and before I knew it, our wedding day had arrived. It was a beautiful ceremony filled with family, friends, and fellow parishioners of the church. As a married woman, I was ready to be a loving and faithful daughter to my God who brought me out of darkness, showed me light and gave me a new life. I will forever be indebted and serve him as long as I live. A faithful, God-fearing, supportive, and caring wife to my husband and a devoted, caring and sacrificing mother to my children. Those were my vows. But deep down, the whisper and sidebar conversations from the so-called congregation, I knew that being a pastor's wife would change my life, attitude, demeanor, character, rights, and make me regret my vows. Something was going to change and it wasn't going to be me. Behind the Closed Doors of Denial!

Chapter 4
Denial

It's been seven years since Mark and I got married and things have been pretty rocky. Since then, our family has grown. I gave birth to our twins, Mona and Mark Jr... They have been a joy in our lives and this coming November, we will be celebrating the twin's second birthday. My father-in-law, Jordan, and my sister-in-law, Annabel, were flying in to be a part of the celebration and to surprise Mark. I had everything ready to start at three o'clock when Mark was expected home.

Everyone was so excited for us and I knew it would make his day to see his family, so we all waited for him to come home. To our surprise, he didn't get home until eleven o'clock. Our twin children's birthday celebration came and went, our family showed up happy and left with a sense of confusion. I was worried after I called his cell phone and no response. I also called the church office and members of the church as I attempted to track him down. When Mark arrived home, he entered the living room and glanced at me on the sofa, but he said nothing to me or the twins. He went straight to his home office.

The next day, Mark did the same thing. No words, no explanation, and no justification for this new behavior. While at the church, he acted like nothing was wrong and I followed suit. I continued to behave like a devoted wife to my husband even though I had no clue as to what had changed in him. When I questioned him about it, he assured me that nothing was wrong and that I was being paranoid about the whole thing.

Maybe I was doing something wrong? Am I not trying my best? Have I been a good wife to my husband? Have I been supportive enough to his ministry? I kept questioning myself as I attempted to figure out what was going on in our marriage. As many questions ran through my mind, I began to feel as if I was being punished for my past. I didn't know what was going on, but I was determined to find out and fix it fast. I knew my husband's schedule 'like the back of my hand,' so I decided to do a surprise visit at the church. Reality slapped me in the face when I walked into his office and found him cheating with Monica, a new member that joined the church a couple of Sundays ago. I told him that she was too extra and always in his face smiling and wearing clothes with no underwear. Disbelief and pain shot through me as I blamed myself for what I had discovered. After all, I was once a woman that slept with married men and now karma was serving me in my coin. I thought I did everything to avoid my past coming back at me but apparently, I didn't do enough. I was being punished for my past mistakes in my present life and I had no choice but to suffer the consequences.

Instead of being upset with Mark for not being faithful to me or our marriage, I was angry at myself for living such a scandalous past. The only way to make things better for our union was for me to forgive my husband for his indiscretions, so I would receive forgiveness from God for my indiscretions. It was the only way for the wounds to heal. I called Lora to help me with this forgiveness process and she told me I should have slapped both of them and cursed them out. But, that would have been my flesh interfering with God's acts of vengeance. We both laughed and the thought did cross my mind. We decided to schedule a girl's weekend away to begin the healing pathway.

Days before the trip to the beach, Mark attempted to apologize for his indiscretions but because I was under the influence of this being my fault, I quickly let him know that he was already forgiven as I wanted to be forgiven for my past. That was the biggest mistake I ever made in this relationship. My need for admonishment had me focusing unnecessarily as I devoted my energy to be a better wife to my husband. I began to question myself about any habits or hang-ups that were keeping me from being a good wife in God's eyes. I did everything that I needed to do to raise my spiritual abilities to meet the demands of my husband, children, and the church. When I looked into the mirror, I wanted to see a strong and worthy God-fearing wife but denial wouldn't allow it. Behind the closed door of denial had me reckless and living a lie.

Lora and I planned to drive together to the ocean view beach resort, but I very much wanted to be alone. So, we decided to meet in the room for lunch at around one o'clock that afternoon. After having that conversation with Mark and catching him with that woman, it triggered something inside of me. Just when I thought I was a butterfly, the caterpillar couldn't forget how to fly. When I arrived at the oceanfront resort that afternoon to check-in, bleary-eyed and distorted, the front desk receptionist gave me the key to room 888. She told me that Lora hasn't arrived and I was eager to spend a few hours alone to gather my thoughts. As I glanced in the reception area, it was bright, beautiful and full of colors. I was so surprised and feeling happy about being near the ocean. I gathered my weekend bag and made plans to enjoy myself and make a good impression on my dear friend, Lora.

From inside the elevator, as it approached the eighth floor, I could hear enraged screaming from inside my soul. It was a tug-of-war going on in my head when I thought about Mark and his lover. As I seized my handbag, it turned upside down, spilling the contents over the elevator floor. I knew right away that my life was upside down and headed for disaster. I gathered my things trying to subdue the panic attack and ran to room 888 before anything else happened. I tried to calm down and realized there wasn't going to be anyone there to help ease the pain. I was in shock and needed some answers. Could it be that I was still in denial? I spent the rest of the day completely wiped out from the combination of stress, depression, shock, and exhaustion. Luckily, when Lora arrived that evening, I had taken a pill to calm my nerves and prepare for a wonderful evening of relaxation. That evening, Lora suggested we have dinner by the water and listen to some jazz music.

"Just what I needed and what the doctor ordered," I said. "Excuse me," Lora replied. "No, I'm just kidding," I said calmly and controlled. "Baby, I'm worried about you," said Lora.

We went to dinner in the lovely Palm Court Jazz café and had an amazing time. I felt drawn to Lora and wanted to erase the memory of seeing them together in my mind and spirit. I did something I knew I wasn't supposed to do, something that went against my beliefs; I ordered a glass of Chardonnay and got up and danced with a stranger. Deep down, I knew it was wrong and could tell that Lora disapproved but she could feel my pain, hurt, sadness, and knew I was having an identity crisis. Lora just sat there, watched me and refused to say a word. After dancing for an hour, Lora was so frustrated, grabbed me off the dance floor and said, "let's take a walk along the ocean."

"Lora, Lora, Lora," I screamed. Why am I in denial? I have no relationship with my family and I never thought I was good enough for Mark and his congregation. I was in denial and thought that this man loved me

if I was a perfectionistic, overachiever, perfect, caring, loving, patient, sensual and kind. No matter what I did, it was never enough for him or those people. When I look in the mirror, I'm overwhelmed, broken, with voids in my life and in danger of losing myself."

The tears started to roll down my face and I knelt in the sand, crying uncontrollably. Lora stopped, knelt, and listened to me to share my pain. It soon became clear to Lora, that I had gained unnecessary weight for caring so much about this man. By helping him discover who he was, N'dia lost who God called her to be in his life. Lora grabbed me and told me to get myself together.

"You are not a basket case and not the only woman in the world whose husband has cheated on her. Any changes in your life can make you vulnerable, but you are too valuable to give up now. *Do you hear me N'dia?*"

I couldn't respond but she nodded by saying yes. Lora grabbed my hands and said this is what we are going to do, as we walked towards the ocean and the waves were moving high. Lora began to speak to the Father in Heaven and tear off generational curses, weights, unforgiveness, identity problems, the lust of the flesh. I could see the heavens open and the sky became light blue. I didn't know what was happening, next, Lora said

"it was time to get baptized from all of my sins. It's your public declaration of your faith in Jesus!"

I didn't know but I wanted to be baptized in the ocean because it is calmer, but symbolic. In the ocean, the waves of hurt and my unforgiveness were trying to knock me down. But, I surrendered to God, felt his Holy Spirit and was surrounded by Lora who was reciting the Lord's prayer, holding me up, and restoring my faith. Lora started to say, "in the name of the Father, Son, and Holy Ghost, I baptize N'dia.

"I knew I wasn't where I wanted to be before Jesus washed away all of my sins and now, I felt like a new person." We cried, celebrated and danced in the ocean just the two of us and the host of heaven. No more denial, no more weight, no more chains, no more sadness, no more emptiness, no more waiting on the world to fill my voids. Jesus had washed all of my sins away.

Chapter 5
People pleasing

Time went on as Mark and I continued living this façade of married life. Every day, I did my best to focus on new responsibilities and challenges that allowed me to forget my life behind closed doors. I was relying on God to keep me stable but the more I ignored the problem, the more it would display itself in not too subtle ways. I felt stuck between two worlds and the excruciating pain I was experiencing was slowly turning me into someone that I didn't want to be. It felt like I was about to lose my character and my mind. There were times where I just wanted him to cuddle me like a baby; instead, he treated me like a stranger in our home. I wanted to hear him utter sweet words of love and affection but instead, all I got from him was that he was too busy to express his love for me. I began to wallow in self-pity; wishing I never got myself into our marriage. Mark was becoming engrossed in his pastoral duties, abandoning his role as a husband and father. He practically locked me out of his world.

In his world, I was an accessory that was just around for the show. There was no excitement between us anymore nor did any of his messages fuel my inspirations. Every Sunday, I watched him preach inspirational words but inside I felt bitter, angry, resentful, and discouraged. How could this man preach about walking on water when he was drowning in the waters of Satan with all of his mistresses? This past 4th Sunday, I was sitting on the first row listening to his message, It was about "Process into Purpose." My tears flowed as I listened keenly and deep down, all of my thoughts were focused on revenge.

I tried hard not to make my thoughts show as he rattled on and the church said *Amen!*

"We are living in a time where the Body of Christ is going through a major shift. Going through a major process of sanctification and accountability," he stated firmly as his eyes swept the congregation. The church said *Amen!* He continued. "God is now calling for the church to come into a greater place of relationship. In this end-time, you are going to have to know that you are saved. The Bible is and has always been fulfilling itself. God is calling for a stronger consecrated life before him. Meaning that we can't go on with the church, as usual, there has to be a change so God can be glorified in your life. *Yes, Lord, I heard a woman from behind me say.*

Many times, we don't understand the process and consequently, some have fallen by the wayside because they could not handle the pressure of the trial.

Often we hear the call but we become afraid of the call because we feel that we are not equipped for the task. God never chooses someone he has not equipped. The process is to assure you remember who called you and anointed you. The process keeps you humble before God, to assure you know it's all about Him. Paul began to demonstrate his humility by saying, "Don't frustrate the grace of God." It's in the process that God begins to shape you and begins to show you who He has made you to be. It's in the process that you learn about you and God begins to reveal Himself to you. The awesome thing about the process is that God knows your ending before your beginning. It's in the process God takes away those things that are not of Him. God needs to see more of Him and less of you and so the process of crucifying yourself with Him now takes place. Sometimes, the process can be a hurting place, a place at times when you just don't understand."

"The process won't kill you, but it will bring you to life," I murmured within myself.

As his first lady, aka supposed to be the only lady, I was experiencing an emotional battle within as I continued my role of people-pleasing; pleasing God, pleasing my children, and pleasing my husband. Where did I lose myself? This process is killing me. I realized that my husband and I have become 'people-driven' where we not only desire other people's attention and love, but we also can't live without it. The only difference between us is how we express it.

After service, I headed over to the pastor's lounge where one of the members of the congregation handed me an envelope.

I was surprised but I smiled and said thank you.

I rushed to my car, quickly got in and opened the letter. It was 3 pages long.

The words penetrated my heart:

Dear First Lady,

I think that an ideal first lady should be one who displays multiple characteristics. She should be poised with self-assured confidence, elegance and graceful mannerisms. She should possess a submissive spirit towards her husband as she is supportive of his ministry. She's also compassionate, toward the people who are in and out of the ministry. She holds a position of strength because the congregation will seek her advice and support. A first lady should have a discerning spirit as many will require her services and she should be able to recognize the needs of the people. A first lady should be patient and live a prayer-filled life, always looking to the Lord for anything and everything. A first lady serves as a mentor, friend, counselor, and an encourager and a motivational speaker to people from all walks of life. She helps with growth in the walk with Christ, the belief and trust in the Lord and the progression of the Christian life.

My family and I at one point only depended on the prayers of others but with the guidance and support from my first lady, my self-esteem has grown. Now, I'm confident in my decision-making and there are big changes in my personal and spiritual life. I still seek her guidance as there's much more work to do but I am confident that God will provide for me.

What I like and admire the most about my first lady is that she is a go-getter. She doesn't let anything hinder her from accomplishing her goals. She's organized, punctual, and knows how to build relationships and takes them to the next level. She's capable of leading others on the path to God and her path is blessed. I'm grateful for her leadership as well as everyone she is involved with. She wants everyone around her to succeed and I continually pray for her as she has helped me change my life for the better.

As I read the letter, the words reopened deep wounds and negative patterns of behaviors that made me feel worse than I did before. I needed to be rescued from my current situation. The double life that I was living was taking a toll on my sanity and I didn't know how to recover from it. My continued façade life was the only thing I knew. This was my life behind closed doors of people-pleasing.

Chapter 6
Frustration

Today, I woke up feeling frustrated and ready to confront my husband about what has been going on with us. I was fed up and I wanted answers. I walked into his home office and started our discussion: *"Mark, did you read the bible verse 1 Timothy 5:8?"*

He looked up from his studies with confusion. I then pulled out my bible to read the verse aloud to him: *"But if any provide not for his own, and especially for those of his own house, he hath denied the faith, and is worse than an infidel."* I looked straight into his eyes and yelled:

"These needs include emotional needs and I shouldn't feel like a stranger in my home!"

I stormed out of his study room as he continued to look confused at my outburst. It seemed to me that he couldn't care less about my feelings. As I was leaving his study room, I heard his cell phone ringing in the living room. I raced down the passageway to get to his phone. He was right on my heels, but I picked up the phone before he could.

Before I could answer, a woman's voice greeted me. *"Hey, baby! Are we still on for tonight?"*

I was still grappling with my response when Mark grabbed the phone out of my hand, ran back into his office and closed the door behind him.

Tears rolled down my cheeks. The perfect marriage that everyone thought I was living was a big lie and my main frustration was that I had to live this life behind closed doors. My soul was overwhelmed with sorrow and depression. I fell to my knees and prayed, "My Father, if it is possible, may this cup be taken from me? Yet, not as I will, but as you will." I decided at the moment that it had to stop and if Mark wasn't going to end this cycle, I certainly planned to.

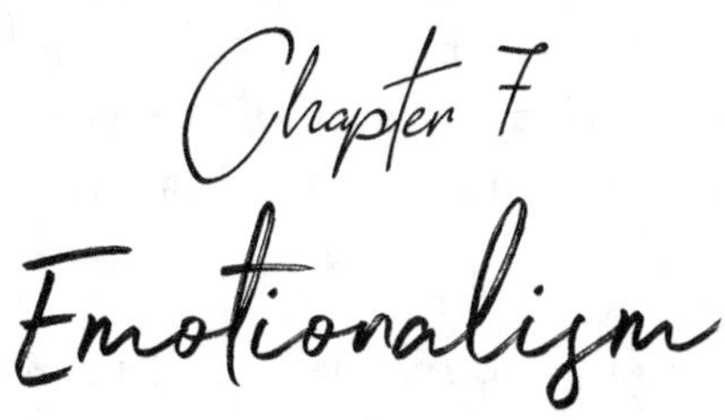

Chapter 7
Emotionalism

Today, as I was hurrying to my favorite coffee Jamaica shop between 5th and 10th street, the feeling of revenge was still within me as I thought about coming up with an action plan. One part of me wanted to stop dwelling on the past, because today, my goal was to begin planning for a better future.

I was trying to find an empty table when a handsome, young man asked me to sit with him. I'm not sure why I agreed to sit with him because I wasn't in the mood of interacting with anyone. My attempts to ignore him did not faze him a bit, he began staring at me instead of reading his newspaper. I tried to ignore him by concentrating on the article I was reading but then my mind began to wander. I started to think about one-night stands and how they were viewed and forgiven differently within relationships. Amazingly enough, I had read that forty-six percent of women indicated that they would forgive their men for a one-night stand and ten percent reported that they would forgive them for long-term affairs. A little voice in my head questioned why I suddenly had thoughts of a one-night stand but at the same time, I couldn't help but think about it because there was a smooth, sexy looking man sitting right across from me. His eyes were drinking in my essence, undressing me with seduction and lust. Although I was pretending to read my article, I could feel him checking me out and as much as I wanted to ignore it, I was excited at the thought of a man wanting me.

Based on his looks and clothing, I figured he was a man of wealth, everything he had on looked like designers. He looked self-assured and I could tell by the service he was getting from the waitress that he was well known in the coffee shop. Sitting in front of this man, I was not only impressed by his demeanor but his mannerisms turned me on. As much as I remind myself that I was a devoted married woman and the first lady of the church, my thoughts ran to and fro about making love with this man. Before I realized what was happening, I had closed my eyes and was visualizing us; his beautiful chocolate skin against mine, his lips on mine. I pictured him looking at me lovingly, and telling me how beautiful I was and how he enjoyed every minute with me. The feelings and emotions of my little daydream were so powerful that I murmured out loud, "the things I would do with you behind closed doors."

His voice brought me back to reality when I heard him say, "Are you talking to me?"

I nervously responded, "Oh no, I'm sorry."

As I gathered my things to leave, he didn't stop me and I was glad because I started sweating, shaking and feeling guilty for thinking such things. I had an interview with Mark Steele who was the president of Whole Foods Co. As I walked out of the coffee shop, I hoped to never see that man again but at the same time, I recognized my strong need for a release.

The distance between the coffee shop and Building 8 was a fifteen-minute commute that I wanted to last for an hour. Building 8 to the Whole Food Corporation was close to several banks, UPS store, and a Trader Joe's. After surveying my surroundings, I glanced at my watch and noticed I was early for my interview, so I took a few minutes to gather myself. My thoughts kept going back to the coffee shop and the handsome man who sat across the table from me. Suddenly, thoughts of Mark cleared everything out of my head. I quickly reminded myself that I was here on business and the only objective was getting this new job. Before I checked in with the receptionist, I headed to the restroom and looked at myself in the mirror. I encouraged myself.

I am a beautiful woman with perfectionist tendencies.

I am the Queen of the kitchen and will bring sunlight to this company.

I am emotionally healthy and capable of doing my daily job responsibilities.

This job will bring a sense of stability and security.

I am a competent woman and claim that this job is mine.

I will not break under pressure and keep God as the center of my life.

I am the best candidate for this position!

With confidence, I smiled at my reflection and headed to the foyer, feeling competent and ready for my new beginning, behind closed doors of emotionalism.

Chapter 8
Restoration

After checking in with the receptionist, she informed me that Mr. Steele was pleased that I was ten minutes early.

"You must be N'dia Brewster," she said excitedly. "You also have an appointment with the executive team at ten, so when you're done meeting with Mr. Steele, I'll have you wait for them in the executive conference room."

This job interview was important to me, especially since I had been watching the company's growth for more than a decade. After having seven interviews, getting rejection letters, and dealing with Mark's behavioral changes, I knew I was going to be blessed with this job. I finally got the opportunity to be introduced to the president of the company and his executive team; nothing was going to deter my success. I researched everything I could to learn more about the executive team as I was eager to impress them and my new boss to be.

"They should be with you in about ten minutes. Would you like a glass of water?" Karen, the receptionist asked me as she escorted me to the executive conference room.

"No, thank you," I replied.

As soon as I sat down in one of the big brown leather chairs in front of the large round table, I admired the beautiful artwork on the wall, wide glass windows, and crystal chandelier. For me, this company and job represented a place of escape from church, my husband, and whomever his next mistress was.

Ten minutes later, there was a knock at the door and the executive team walked into the conference room, sat, and introductions began. I tried to remember their names as they spoke—Tom, David, Brenda, Lila, Matthew, Ricky, April, and Mark Steele. I extended my hand as I greeted each of them. Karen quickly rolled in a tray with coffee and breakfast goodies for the team and everyone grabbed something from the tray except for me.

I nervously settled into the chair and looked around the room while the executive team reviewed my resume. As I surveyed everyone in the room, I realized that the man sitting next to Mr. Steele was the same man that sat across from me in the coffee shop. I wasn't sure how I didn't realize it when he walked into the room, but at that point, it was too late. He was here and I was too. I waited patiently for the questions to start rolling in.

"How about you start by telling us all about yourself and your interest in the company?" Mr. Steele said.

As I responded to his question, I noticed the team jotting down my responses. I did my best to convey positive communication while displaying confidence in myself and my abilities. With every answer, I made it clear that I was the right person for the job. As the new Senior Executive Project Analyst, I made it clear that I could assist them with setting a clear direction, aligning the team with business goals, and motivating and inspiring the organization to achieve long-term strategic initiatives. Even though I was concentrating on winning everyone over, I couldn't help but notice Matthew Resto's demeanor. He hardly spoke but when he did, his words were electrifying to me. He was more than just eye candy. His position as the VP of Operations kept him very busy. My professional demeanor melted a bit when he spoke.

"N'dia, I'm very impressed with your responses and your skills are impeccable. I have only one question for you to make my decision."

My legs began to shake, and my mind started to race. I watched his lips as they formulated the words and my anxiety level shot upwards. My heart was pounding, and nervous sweat ran down my back. I reminded myself that I was in an interview and the thoughts of being attracted to this man had to go.

Finally, I managed to say, "What would you like to know?"

"Behind closed doors, are you a leader or a follower?" Matthew asked.

"I'm a leader, Mr. Resto. All you have to do is give me a chance and I'll prove it to you!" I responded with confidence and a bit of raw sexuality. My heart pounded even louder because I had no idea where that came from.

A little voice in my head told me that I was in for a long and rough ride with this company…and Matthew Resto, behind the open doors of restoration.

Chapter 9
Revenge

As the newly appointed Senior Executive Project Analyst, I knew that I had a rough journey ahead of me before I got completely comfortable in my position. My ninety days performance review was fast approaching, and Matthew Resto was my immediate manager. The previous manager had made a mess of the previous ten projects and my biggest strength was collaboration and organization. Leadership was one of the most important skills in my position and I did my best to execute it with every duty given to me. To build trust and strengthen my team, I had to be relentless with delegating tasks on the projects to avoid burnout.

My interaction with my new boss was amazing yet uncomfortable at times. We both worked hard and kept everything professional but there were moments where we both felt sexual chemistry between us. Matthew loved the fact that I was able to motivate the team to get positive results, therefore, helping to fulfill the strategic goals of the company. I was the first to arrive and last to leave every night because I wanted to be successful at my job and I wanted to be part of the company's growing success. Things at home were still the same so I concentrated on my work life. I avoided any interaction with Matthew that may seem sexual or flirtatious.

Finally, it was time to do and discuss my performance review. I was sitting in Matthew's office waiting for him to begin the review when I noticed that he had no pictures anywhere. Once he was done reviewing the paperwork in front of him, he looked up at me and smiled. I absolutely loved his smile.

"You look very nice today," he said.

"Thank you so much," I replied. It made me happy that he noticed my new skinny outfit.

"You're welcome. I did want to discuss a problem with you, a problem that you're not aware of." The disappointment in his eyes was clear as I've seen that look before. Mark had that look in his eyes every time we spoke.

"The staff morale has gone up and productivity is at an all-time high, yet there's an unavoidable problem among us."

I was confused but I tried not to show it. I was hoping that this problem had nothing to do with me or my performance review.

"I'm not quite sure what you mean Matthew," I said.

"Before you started here, the company was on the verge of closing for good but all of the projects and duties you've been assigned have been successful. Everything you've done so far has been for the betterment of the company and we're now flourishing. It is a great thing and I thank you for being a part of the company's latest successes. The problem in the midst is that I feel you're keeping pieces of information to yourself that needs to be shared. I have a question for you. Have you been keeping important information to yourself? Information that you know you should be sharing with a colleague or even me?" Matthew asked.

I stared at him for a moment because I was very confused by his questions.

"I have done that in the past to protect the colleague and myself," I said.

"Do you think that's fair?" He said.

"It's not about being fair as it is more about doing the right thing," I said.

"So you think it's right that we have feelings for each other and not share them? That we continue to work together side by side and not acknowledge our true feelings?" he said.

I was thinking about the company's policies but my flesh was screaming for the attention.

I had no response as thoughts were racing in my head. Matthew continued. "We both felt a spark between us from the first day you sat across the table from me in the coffee shop. I don't want to ignore my feelings and neither should you," I know you're not happy in your marriage, he said.

I stared at the floor to avoid looking at him. I worked so hard to hide my feelings and ignore what was going on between us but not once did I think that he would confront me about this. I was shocked, confused, and didn't know what my next move was.

"I want you to spend the night with me," he said quietly.

My head jerked up and I felt my lips trembling.

If Matthew noticed the change in my demeanor, he did not react to it. "My driver will pick you up at 8 pm and we'll have an intimate dinner. How does that sound?"

Matthew's question had me in the hot seat and I didn't know what to say. Part of me couldn't believe this was happening, another part of me reminded me of the fact that I was married; therefore I shouldn't entertain his request. Then I remembered that my 'pastor husband' was cheating on me every second of my life and he cared less about my feelings about it. Right then and there, I decided to think about me and only me.

"That does sound wonderful but as far as my accepting your offer, that depends," I said.

"Depends on what exactly?" he said.

"It depends on how well my performance review goes," I replied jokingly to lighten the mood of the room."

"Beauty and a sense of humor are the make-up of a perfect woman. Something tells me that once I have you, I'll never let you go. Do you feel it too?" Matthew leaned in and whispered to me.

His words caused tingles to rush down my spine, touched me in all the right spots and woke up a craving that I haven't had in a long time. Even though I tried to avoid it, I knew this was going to happen from the minute I sat across from him in the coffee shop.

I was well aware that a married woman shouldn't be having sexual thoughts for another man but my 'pastor husband' never thought about my feelings when he was sleeping with his mistresses, so why should I? I wasn't ready to admit it out loud, but not only did I want this man badly, but I also wanted to show him how badly I wanted him behind closed doors of revenge.

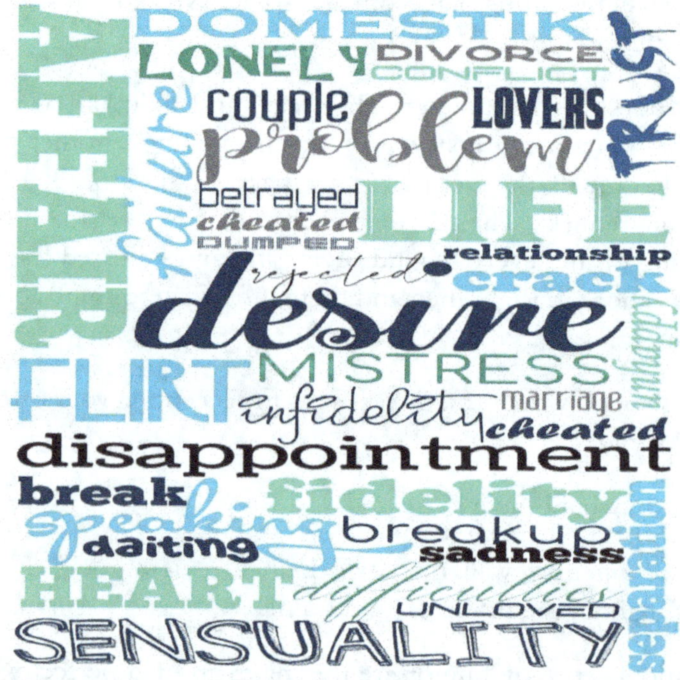

Chapter 10
Intimacy

As I sipped my coffee, I thought about my current situation. I was in a loveless marriage with Mark and falling in love with Matthew. Mark couldn't care less about the amount of time I spent at work nor did he notice the change in my behavior. I felt younger, refreshed, and confident as my work life was fulfilling all of my needs, wants, and desires.

After several months, I learned that Matthew had no children, he was a fraternal twin and was given up for adoption at a young age. He didn't know anything about his brother and recently, he had hired an investigator to locate his missing brother named Mark. Matthew's life was pretty simple, and I have to say I was glad to be a part of it.

When Matthew and I were together, it felt like exodus to me. It was like an undesirable fire in my bod. He made love to me constantly like he was my husband and treated me with love and respect. The treatment and affection I was looking for from my husband, I was getting from my lover. Deep down, I knew it was wrong to be cheating on my husband. The fact that he was cheating as well didn't make what I was doing right…

but it felt so good that I couldn't avoid wanting Matthew. Every time he touched me, I melted. Every kiss felt like a God-sent gift. Every whisper of love vibrated through our bodies. Wanton and decadent sex between two people that loves and appreciates each other is what we got from each other. Matthew always took the time out to please me and make sure I was pleased in every way. I found so much pleasure in pleasing him as I gave him all of me. Our sexual union was always magical, enticing, and electrifying. My life was better because of him and all that we did behind closed doors of intimacy.

Chapter 11
Guilt

As Matthew and I continued to spend more time together, a sense of guilt grew within me that I couldn't avoid. As far as my job was concerned, things were great as I moved up in the company and was traveling about ninety percent of the time. As much as I enjoyed my double life, my conscience let me know that it was the wrong way to go. What I didn't know was that things were going to change for the worse. It all started when I was called to Matthew's office for an emergency meeting. Once I arrived, he called Mark Steele and put the phone on speaker.

Mark didn't even greet us, he just got right to the point of his call. "I got a message earlier today about you. Apparently, this person has some damaging information about you Matthew and is threatening to expose you and your multiple relationships with women in the company. This person claims to have pictures of sexual acts, proof of video footage about your use of drugs, that you have a drinking problem. If revealed, all of this information can become very damaging to the company's reputation, not to mention that we could be sued and lose millions of dollars. I have no choice but to let you go, Matthew. I'm sorry it had to be this way but at the same time I cannot allow you to work here after all that has happened."

As I was listening to the news, I was crushed and immediately ran to the bathroom to throw up. I couldn't believe that I was going through this with Matthew nor did I want to accept that everything we had been through was crushed by the weight of this news.

Mr. Steele's words were still ringing in my ears. "N'dia will take over your position going forward and we will work quickly and diligently to clean up the mess you've made and restore the company's reputation. Again, Matthew, I'm sorry it had to be like this but please do clear out your office and leave immediately."

I felt sorry for myself behind closed doors of guilt.

Chapter 12

Misery

The next few months were the hardest for me as the new vice president of Operations. My career was at an all-time high until I got some not-so-welcoming news at my latest GYN appointment. According to Doctor Reginald, I was pregnant. I hadn't been intimate with Mark in months so I knew I had to come up with a plan to hide my mistake. I coerced Mark to have sex with me even though all of my thoughts were on Matthew. The twins were now approaching age 5 and I was pregnant.

This past Sunday, I was sitting in church with my big pink hat thinking about being rescued from my situation. I wanted to run to the church altar and whisper the prayer my grandmother always recited to me. Yes, I grew up on Psalm 86: 6– 9, and I can hear it playing in my mind.

"Give ear, O LORD, unto my prayer; and attend to the voice of my supplications. In the day of my trouble I will call upon thee: for thou wilt answer me. Among the gods there is none like unto thee, O Lord; neither are there any works like unto thy works. All nations whom thou hast made shall come and worship before thee, O Lord; and shall glorify thy name. [Psalm 86:6-9].

The tears began to flow when the choir started singing "Lord I Need Your Help."

The church was full of people, yet I felt alone as my husband walked past me and headed for the pulpit. His sermon this morning was about "getting the thief out of your house."

The thief that steals your joy, makes you doubt God and his role in your life. He instructed the church to open their Bibles to the key Scriptures - Isaiah 10:27 and St. John 10:9-10. As he expounded on the Scriptures, I took notes.

We are in a time where the enemy is trying to steal everything from the children of God.

The enemy desires to keep a yoke around the neck of the children of God.

Yokes are things that keep your focus off the will and plan of God.

Many of us are seeking to go to higher levels in the Lord but because of circumstances, it seems as though we get into a place of complacency.

Being complacent is a place where you as a child of God never want to be in.

There are times when God has you at a standstill so that you will trust him. But then, there are times when Satan has created obstacles that battle your spirit.

If the enemy can hinder you through circumstances, he feels as though he has done his job.

We are moving into a season of abundance, but this season requires you to surrender all to God.

Faith is the vehicle that moves God.

To move in God, you have to operate in faith, and the only way your faith will grow is by hearing, believing, and working the Word of God.

Many times we are out of position for the blessing because of sin.

Sin will keep you in a place of lack and a place of suffering.

There are trials that God allows us to go through but then there are trials that we create ourselves.

And so, it is important to understand that the next level of Glory is going to require Holiness, it is time to be delivered from the sin that has had you bound.

Touch your neighbor and tell them I am no longer bound, I am free through the POWER OF GOD!!!!!

All that Mark was saying spoke to me, deep in my soul and heart, behind closed doors of misery.

Chapter 13

Transparency

I sat on the brown corduroy material sofa and my body sunk into the cushion. The couch hugged her, and she moved about to get comfortable. Her patent leather boot made the sound of two balloons being rub together every time she crossed her legs.

"Mrs. N'dia," the receptionist who sat behind a glass window and large desk called her name. She fought with the sofa and her patent leather boots to get up. Finally, out of the chair, she sashayed over to the window.

"Dr. Reece will be with you shortly. You're next."

N'dia rolled her eyes at the woman and went back to her seat.

In the meantime, Dr. Reece read over N'dia's Chart.

The patient is diagnosed with Schizophreniform Disorder. The patient has had seven previous hospitalizations and during that time, the patient had a severe hypomanic episode where she was reported by her mother as extremely agitated, talking excessively, climbing on furniture, yelling profanity, and was reported as becoming psychically and verbally aggressive. The patient was brought in on hold by the Law Enforcement. Previous diagnosis of Bipolar I Disorder. The patient has paranoid delusions, thoughts, hallucinations, and displays disorganized behaviors. The patient also has a history with narcissism that dictates gratification and attention. The patient has a long history of various psychiatrist changes. The patient has been prescribed [add psychotropic drugs for schizophrenia]. The patient often refuses meds and has had several psychotic episodes when off meds. The patient has a long outstanding history with aggression and psychical violence. The patient appeared progressively psychotic, agitated and reported severe insomnia.

The doctor will see you now," announced the receptionist. Dr. Reese's colorful tie laid neatly over his white button-down, neatly pressed shirt. The man's face was stoic, but he mustered up a smile to greet N'dia his longest-running patient. His belly hung slightly over his pants and beads of sweat sat on his forehead.

N'dia was still annoyed so she slammed the magazine she was reading on the small table beside her before fighting to get off the sofa.

Dr. David Reese, based on my interactions with him was a short stocky Christian man with glasses, he stood in the doorway of his office watching N'dia trying to balance her way to him in her boots. She grimaced, reminding herself that the boots were clearly too tall for her to be wearing in her state.

"Dr. Reese," N'dia greeted him coldly and sashayed past him and into the office. She took in the large window overlooking the city skyline. *The view is beautiful,* she thought, before taking a deep breath and flopping down on the light blue plush love seat before Dr. Reese's desk.

"Hi, N'dia, how are you today?" Dr. Reese's mood seemed to lighten as he closed the door and made his way to his seat behind his large oak wood desk. He looked over at the picture of his wife of 20 years in front of him before glancing over his glasses at me. I noticed that he shook his head to focus on his professionalism and recited his oath he took as a doctor so many years ago.

"So N'dia, tell me how you've been?"

"Horrible, Doctor!"

Dr. Reese sat back as if preparing himself for the wave of the rants he encountered so many times.

"What's going on exactly?" Dr. Reese asked, peering over the top of his glasses rims while jotting down notes on his note pad.

"Well Doctor, I was confronted by another of my husband's mistresses and my lover has abandoned me with his baby! Can you believe she had the nerve to confront me? Do you believe she had the nerve to tell me that my *affair* with my husband has to stop? Who does she think she is? She can't tell me what to do with my husband!"

"You need to calm down, getting this upset while pregnant is not good for the baby's health," Dr. Reece cautioned.

"I do need to calm down," I said, more so to myself. My voice served as a calming gesture, but I could not slow down or stop. I wanted to share what happened when I met with yet another of my husband's mistresses for dinner.

"This new mistress, I call her number ten, arranged to meet me at the Lifetime gym. I decided to meet there to avoid seeing anyone who knows me. I was embarrassed enough by her actions. This particular mistress was much younger and bolder than the rest of them. She wanted to expose the intimate details of their affair to the world and I can't let that happen. She had laid out their elaborate affair in full detail and if this information is exposed, not only will I look like a fool, my husband's reputation will be forever tarnished. Why should I care? Because HE'S MY HUSBAND! NO ONE ELSE GETS HIM BUT ME! I guess she expected that by telling me this, I would leave my husband. That's not going to happen. These women have a lot of things in common, they love any man that has leadership and power."

"Why do you believe that N'dia?" Dr. Reece paused to ask a question.

"Satan himself! But honestly, I'm not sure," I continued. "My first experience with a man of power involved so much pain, Dr. Reece. I guess over the years, the time I spent not only acknowledging it privately but also condoning it made me feel that it would stop happening eventually. I felt that was the solution to all of the problems and what most leading ladies with men in this position deal with. Number ten claimed that she was reaping the benefits of my failing marriage. She described Mark as being weak-minded and needed fun. She also said that he needed a loving, bossy, adventurous, and daring woman in his life. She said he was easy to spot because his fake toughness made people think that he had it all together."

Dr. Reese interjected again, "N'dia help me understand. Why do you feel the need to meet with these women? Better yet, why do you only blame the mistresses and not hold your husband accountable for his actions? Do you truly believe that meeting with these women will make your husband's infidelity disappear and somehow he'll be the husband you want and need?"

"Exactly! My power is that I'm still married to him, he's mine. I've got what they want, and I will not give it up! I'm showing my husband that I'm his loyal wife no matter what and no power-hungry mistress will take that away! I don't know any other way to gain back my power, plus, I have a secret that I'm sure he will never forgive, so for financial stability and my family, I will stay with my husband and the church."

As I continued my rant, I recalled yet another letter I received from a woman in our congregation:

Dear First Lady,

The term First Lady is often romanticized as one with special privileges. The church often extends this title to the wife of their shepherd. This denotes the first family as above the other families of the congregation. While many women feel it is an honor to be married to the Pastor of the church, most pastors' wives feel anything but first. Romans 13:7 tells us to give respect and honor to whom it's due but we must be careful not to worship or idolize God's men and women as if they're little gods. A real first lady doesn't seek the title but is called to it!

So, what is an ideal First Lady? She is the epitome of the Proverbs 31 woman. Her husband knows she can be trusted. She not only supports him and his calling for ministry, but she recognizes her calling as well. The call started the moment she said, "I do" to the Pastor or the moment her husband became a pastor. She cares for things that are of eternal value. She isn't impressed by things of momentary value or having her ears filled with chatter. Oftentimes, she's up praying for the people of the congregation when others are sound asleep. She is frequently seen standing by her husband's side in the light but when outside of the light, she works tirelessly behind the scenes to make sure everything goes effortlessly when the doors of the church are opened. Her light never burns dim or goes out in the night. She doesn't trust in her strength but draws her strength from the Lord. Selfless, not selfish, she loves unconditionally and has no problem laying her needs aside to help others. She makes sure everyone feels part of the spiritual family.

Finally, she hopes and perseveres until the end and doesn't allow mistakes or unforgiveness to enter into the camp because she recognizes that God's grace is the reason why she was put into this place. She has to be happy with who she is and blossom in her position. I love you First Lady N'dia!

Love, Felicia

MCBC Woman's President

"N'dia, you have to know that everything around you is showing you signs of what you need to do to be healthy. These are signs you have to pay attention to for your sanity and the good of the baby," Dr. Reese said.

"I will admit that lately, everything has been catching up with me. I have been feeling fatigued and having difficulty concentrating," I confessed.

"Are you taking your medication?" Dr. Reese asked, looking at me squarely in the eyes.

"Yes, unfortunately, I hate those little pills and I stopped taking them because of my pregnancy."

"N'dia, it's important you stick with the medication plan. You have been functioning relatively well compared to your past episodes. Do you see the connection between your meds and your current health?"

"Doctor, I don't want to talk about those crazy pills."

"What do you want to talk about then?" Dr. Reese said.

"I want to finish telling you about mistress number 10 and my secret lover, Mark."

"Okay, N'dia," said Dr. Reese with some trepidation in his tone. He was looking at his clock. The clock said 11:45 am. Their hour session was about to come to an end.

My rant continued. "In life, I came to realize that being a first lady is about influence and having the ability to exercise my influence behind closed doors. Behind closed doors, these mistresses are thirsty for pleasure from married men. Behind closed doors, they fantasize about how to engage strong but weak men of power into their webs of deception and there's no way I will allow any of his mistresses to win!"

The bell rang to let both of us know that the counseling session was over.

Dr. Reece smiled and said, "I'll see you next week!" Let's discuss behind the closed door of transparency.

Chapter 14

Practice what you preach!

I decided, after my last counseling session with Dr. Reese, I had to tell Mark I was pregnant with our third child. My motivation for sharing this news at this time was that the church was celebrating its 21st anniversary. Mark's mind was on his pastoral duties and entertaining all of the guest speakers from all over the world. I kept reciting this Scripture Ps. 37:23-24, *"The steps of a good man are ordered by the Lord and He delights in his way. Though he falls [righteous people can fail, or fall, or be discouraged, etc.], he shall not be utterly cast down; FOR [it's a big FOR!] THE LORD UPHOLDS HIM WITH HIS HAND."*

At the same time, as I was about to reveal this, I felt so blind and unable or unwilling to discern or make sound decisions. Quite simply, I needed guidance, direction, and someone to help formulate what I needed to do next. I had so many habits, hang-ups and had experienced so much hurts I had allowed festering. I felt like I was bleeding. My life was slowly heading for disaster in almost every area.

For the next twenty days straight, I went to the coffee shop hoping to run into Matthew. I didn't. I continuously pondered—*Will he forgive me? Would he ever want to touch me, even if it was for the last time?* I needed to feel his arms around me just one last time.

The anxiousness that developed in me as I hoped to see him made me feel nauseated, so I told myself to calm down, grab a seat near a window, and have a muffin. While I waited in line to place my order, I noticed a man who was very familiar from behind me eating with a beautiful woman dressed in red. I realized the man was my husband with mistress number ten. The cheating piece of a man told me that he had a Pentecostal board meeting and would see me at the 7:30 church service.

"Once a cheat, always a cheat," I murmured to myself. No matter what I did to get rid of these women, he found a way to add more to the pile, but today was going to be the last day. My husband, Pastor Mark, was getting too used to having his cake and eating it, but not this time. Today was the day he was going to pay for his indiscretions. It was time for him to practice what he preached! I wasn't sure if it was the pregnancy hormones or missing Matthew or the ideal first lady letters that prompted me, but I walked towards the table and started shouting at both of them.

"No matter what I do to get rid of your easy lays, you still find a way to get another one! You have no respect for me, our marriage, our children and the words you preach every Sunday! Every time you get in bed with filthy whores, it makes you just as bad as they are!"

My eyes felt like they were going to burst from my sockets, the rage in my body and the tone of my voice scared me. I could tell by the way Mark and his mistress were gaping at me, that they were shocked to see me, and the words that were coming from my mouth.

Mark attempted to calm me down. "Let's go somewhere behind closed doors to discuss this."

I refused. I was on a roll that I should've been on long ago and nothing he said was going to stop me.

"Shut the hell up, Mark! You bastard! Go to hell and take all your nasty whores with you! You are a nasty, low down, dirty, lying, cheating, insecure bastard! I hate you! I can't do this anymore with you! You've continuously hurt me to my core and I'm finally done with your trifling behind!"

When I made my last statements, I kicked him as hard as I could between his legs. Once he was down on his knees, I began to whoop him like he stole something. I let out all of my frustrations with every punch and kick. The mistress had a problem with him too because she joined me in beating him.

Mark was getting so many punches and kicks, he didn't know what to do with himself. Every time he tried to block or stop a hit another one would surprise him. People around us did their best to pull us off him but what they didn't know was that I had years of hurt built up, I wanted him to die just like my heart did ten years ago. It wasn't the pastor I was trying to kill, I was trying to kill the man that took my life away from me. Deep down, I loved him but knew it was time he practiced what he preached and get the thief out of his life.

"N'dia and Kontastia, please stop! What the hell are you thinking?" Mark shouted as he grimaced in pain.

I felt my heart rate spiking as sweat was pouring down my back. Yet as soon as I heard him call out her name my blood pressure rose.

Suddenly, an unpleasant feeling came over me. My nose started bleeding, adrenaline rushed to my brain and all the anger I felt towards Mark, his mistresses and the continuous embarrassment over the years had me spinning out of control. Next thing I knew, I fainted. Before I was totally out of it, I heard Mark and Matthew calling my name.

Chapter 15

Ultimatums

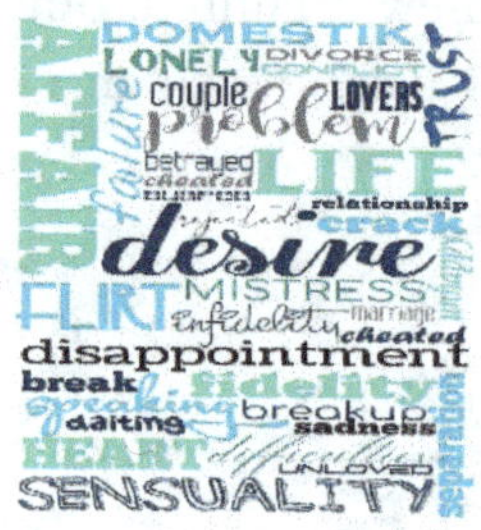
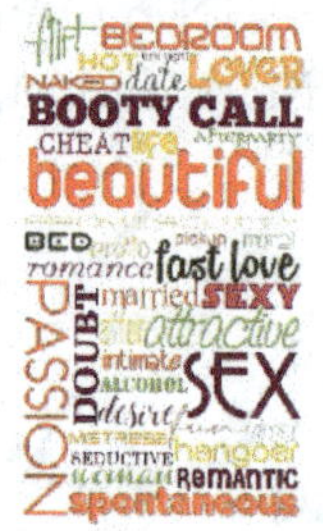
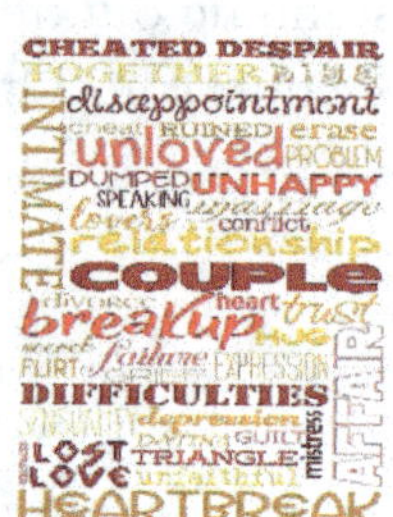

As I laid in my bed at the Rex Hospital, images of the heartache that I had been through flowed through my mind. They thought I was unconscious, but I heard everything the doctors discussed with Mark, Matthew, my parents and Karen, my best friend. The words, "the baby and mom were in critical but stable condition," kept ringing in my head. Mark and Matthew were in complete denial concerning the news of my pregnancy. With squinted eyes, I could see their faces at my bedside, but I didn't want to acknowledge nor face the reality of the situation. The whole game of hiding extramarital affairs, meeting with the mistresses, my revenge tryst and thrill were finally over. No more playing around with my future. The grace of God kept me alive for a reason and I need to stand by my man. Now the question was, which man? Mark or Matthew.

When I was with Matthew, he not only treated me like he loved me, but he also made me feel important and wanted. I was his one and only. With Mark, I was the woman he wanted to be with for the sake of the church. Matthew gave me self-confidence, great love-making, and personal attention. Mark, on his good days, made people feel good about themselves and their journey with God. Despite his adulterous ways, he did provide our home with stability, security, and nurturing for our children. Not only did I want to forgive Mark, but I also wanted to forgive Matthew and myself for any part we played in these affairs. Soon, everyone exited the room. I was staring at their retreating backs when I realized that Mark was still in the room.

His watery eyes fell on my body before he fell to knees and began praying. I listened keenly.

"My God, why has thou forsaken me? Help my dearest N'dia and our unborn baby. N'dia, please wake up, don't leave me. N'dia, I'm so sorry for all the hurt and pain that I've caused you over the last ten years. In my mind, publicly my heart was in the marriage but privately, I lost sight of who we were or who God wanted me to be. While I was committing adultery, I subconsciously believed I wasn't doing anything wrong. I believed all the lies I told myself and I continued my actions while thinking that it wouldn't affect you. I believed that no matter what I did with those mistresses, you would never leave me nor would my actions outside of our home affect us inside. I was so wrong N'dia, and I'm truly sorry. I made you feel like my desire for the flesh was more important than our marriage and I'm so sorry my love. I should've realized how bad it was getting once you started taking those pills and going to those counseling sessions, but I was so into my pleasures that I completely forgot about yours. Please, God, have mercy on me," Mark murmured as he lowered his head even further.

"Give me another chance to love this woman as I should. I repent because I disregarded her feelings, and hid the fact that I found my missing brother. I repent for paying for all of the abortions my mistresses had because of me. I repent for not being the husband that my wife deserves for all of these years. Lord, I repent and I'm asking for you to have mercy on me; please allow me to keep my family, wife, church, and my unborn baby. Lord, take this thorn away from me. I'm vulnerable, insecure, weak, and scared."

Mark was crying like a baby while clutching my hand.

"Set me free and I promise to take better care of my wife, your church, and my children. Please God, this is my sincere promise and vow to thee," Mark declared.

I whispered in response, "I'm here Mark, please take me home."

As Mark cried out, Matthew burst into the room to see what was going on. As soon as he saw my eyes open, he ran over to me and gave me a big hug.

"N'dia, I love you," Matthew said after releasing me. "I'm so glad you're awake. Is that my baby?"

I couldn't face him; I fainted immediately. All I remembered was Matthew shouting, "Get the doctor now!"

What did you think about Pastor Mark and N'dia's relationship? What were some deal breakers for you?

____

____

____

Do you think Mark was intimidated by N'dia?

____

____

____

Do you think N'dia will have the courage to move on or stay in her marriage?

____

____

____

Private Collection of Poetry

Behind the Closed Doors of Church is hard to describe.

Lord, help me get over me and allow me to share my mind

My mind is about to go Snapple, crack and pop

My husband loves You and serves his mistress too

What am I supposed to do?

Where do I go, can anyone see that I am blue

One thing about being blue

Is that you never know

What God has in store for you to do.

I married a man, and this was not part of the plan

Church, Mistress and Dealing with the Man

The Man of God and the Man of the Night

When did all this happen and it's clouding me with all of my might?

Behind Closed Doors thoughts of pain

Misery loves company, but so does pain

Pain has a way of dealing with your heart

But so does God and He will give me a new start

Behind Closed Doors

There is a Sequel Coming

What do you want or can you see what's coming?

Ndia, Mark or her ongoing boo

What do you want N'dia to do?

Love, Leave or Last it out

Email me your thoughts and you will have to
wait

This one out!

Behind Closed Doors

Dr. Richelle L. Resto is a native of Durham, North Carolina, and is the Executive Pastor of Dominion Cathedral Ministry in Maryland. She is a graduate of North Carolina Central University, Capella University, and Isaiah Seminary College. She is a respected educational, community, and spiritual leader that continues to impart lifelong realistic strategies that promote discipline, balance, endurance, and opportunities.

SYNOPSIS:

Many times, Pastors in leadership positions have many roles inside and outside the church. They tend to enjoy having the applauses in the church, but ignore the silent ones that come from the people at home. Pastor Mark lived his life to the fullest, loved the applause, attention of the women and all of the bells and whistles that came from the congregation. Behind Closed Doors, he had deep secrets, demons, that made him struggle to deal with the thorns in his flesh, and all of his mistresses. N'dia, the lovely first lady, is fighting internal struggles and finds herself in the web of indecisions, even considering herself as one of the mistresses. Behind Closed Doors, N'dia had had to learn how to triumph over years of pain, fight through the tears, and overcome turmoils as being the Leading First Lady. While dealing with the reality that her husband was married to the church and left her to deal with all of his mistresses. This book shares vital information about things that happen Behind the Closed Doors of Pastors, Pastor's wives, and all of their mistresses.

For inquiries, visit the website
and social media platforms below

WEBSITE: www.drresto.org

FACEBOOK: facebook.com/authorrichelleresto

INSTAGRAM: dr.resto